IN THE EARLY DAYS of the Covid-19 pandemic, the world turned inside out. Around the globe, people stayed inside or kept close to home, going out only for essentials or because they had to do essential work. Schools and businesses closed. Airplane flights were canceled. Cars stayed parked, boats anchored. Air, light, and noise pollution decreased. The skies, roads, and waterways were more clear and quiet. As a result, the natural world seemed to return to an earlier, wilder state.

For scientists and conservationists, this moment became an unplanned experiment. What would happen to wildlife while human activity paused?

What happened is this: Animals ventured out into the human-free places. They crossed boundaries that people had set for them in the past few centuries. They reclaimed ancient habitats as their own—temporarily, at least.

Here are some of their stories.

For Paul, Leo, Pietro, and Milo, who shared the anthropause with me in Brooklyn; with special thanks to the people who kept our city alive until we heard the birds sing louder than sirens. And for my parents, who made sure this city girl got out into nature.

—L.T.

With this book, I would like to say "thank you" to all those who work tirelessly, even during the difficult times of the pandemic, to ensure that tomorrow and in the future we will still find an intact nature in which we can observe wild animals in their natural habitat.

    Let's all do our part.

—A.S.

minedition

A division of Astra Publishing House
North American edition published 2021 by mineditionUS

Text copyright © by Lenora Todaro 2021
Illustrations copyright © by Annika Siems 2021
Coproduction with minedition Ltd., Hong Kong
Rights arranged with "minedition ag", Zurich, Switzerland. All rights reserved.

mineditionUS, 19 West 21st Street, #1201, New York, NY 10010
e-mail: info@minedition.com
This book was edited by Leonard Marcus and Maria Russo
and printed in May 2021 at Grafiche AZ, Verona (BA), Italy
Typesetting in Times Roman
Library of Congress Cataloging-in-Publication Data available upon request.

ISBN 978-1-6626-5049-9
10 9 8 7 6 5 4 3 2 1
First Impression

For more information please visit our website: www.minedition.com

Lenora Todaro

SEA LIONS IN THE PARKING LOT

Animals on the Move in a Time of Pandemic

Illustrated by Annika Siems

minedition

a maria russo book

1.

The parklands of Adelaide, Australia, form a figure eight, wrapping the city center with a green belt. Mobs of kangaroos live nearby in the hills among the shrubbery and woods. Usually, they don't go into the city. It's crowded with people and cars. Scary, for a roo.

When the people of Adelaide stay inside, the city is quiet. One morning, a kangaroo leaves its home and enters the city's center. Like a fugitive, it bounces down empty avenues, bounds through stop lights, free to hop here and there and everywhere.

2.

A herd of Sika deer amble boisterously around a park in Nara, Japan. Local residents and tourists like to feed the deer "shika senbai," specially cooked crackers. The deer love this snack. Sometimes, though, they swallow discarded wrappers and plastic bags that are fragrant with the smell of human food. Then they feel sick.

With the people inside, there are few crackers to be found in the park, and fewer plastic wrappers, too. Hungry, the deer munch juicy leaves and grass in the park. Delish! But they want more. They venture out of the park, bowing their heads to nibble on potted plants as they pad through the city. Their bellies feel so good that they go for a romp in the subway, hooves hitting the platform like wooden blocks.

3.

Most of the world's giant pandas live in bamboo forests in the mountains of central China. They are usually solitary animals, but when a group of pandas does come together, they are known by a funny name: a cupboard. There are not that many wild pandas left in the world—fewer than 2,000—because of climate change and habitat loss, and because it's tricky for a panda to get pregnant. A female panda can conceive only during one to three days in the spring. When a baby panda is born in captivity at a zoo, it is cause for celebration.

    With the zoos closed, the pandas have privacy from noisy crowds. At Ocean Park in Hong Kong, Ying Ying and Le Le mate for the first time in ten years. In a theme park not far from Seoul, South Korea, Ai Bao and Le Bao give birth to the first panda cub ever born in that country.

4.

In the shadows of towering buildings, a flamboyance of flamingos roost and nest in the wetlands of Navi Mumbai in India. Wetlands are like sponges, helping to control floods. Wetlands are home to so many creatures and plants and trees. Flamingos migrate here every year.

Undisturbed by people, fishing boats, and construction, flamingos forage for algae and other tiny organisms. So much good food is easy to get now. More flamingos than usual flock to the area —nearly 150,000! As they lift into the sky, they paint the water pink.

5.

Sea turtles have lived in the world's oceans since the age of dinosaurs, swimming and tending to coral and seagrass along the way. When it's time to lay eggs, they return to the beaches where they were born. Often turtle eggs hatch simultaneously, and suddenly the beach is full of newborns.

With the coastlines deserted, these seafaring reptiles nest and hatch in record numbers. Their beaches are dark at night and uncrowded in the day. Vessel-free waters make swimming a breeze.

In Mexico's Sonora State, the indigenous Seri community monitors more than 2,000 newborn olive ridley sea turtles, compared to the more usual 500. The hatchlings hoist their heart-shaped shells to the sky and tiptoe their way into the Gulf of California. A bale of ninety-seven hawksbill sea turtles hatch on an abandoned beach in Brazil. They navigate by the slope of the sand, and the brightest direction. When the night sky spills its reflection onto the water, they march their two-inch-long bodies into the Atlantic Ocean.

6.

A pride of lions lounge on a barren road in the South African savanna—grasslands where lone trees have popped up here and there. Ordinarily, the roads are clogged with safari trucks filled with tourists wielding cameras and phones. All the human activity nudges the lions deeper into the bush, especially in daytime.

What a relief it is for the lions to be able to laze on a warm road, to yawn and snooze with their bellies full in the hot midday sun, without bother from growling vehicles and chatty onlookers.

7.

You can hear a troop of mountain gorillas before you see them. They chomp on leaves in the forest canopy. Then one slips down a tree, and you see a flicker of black fur. Uganda's mist-shrouded slopes and dense rainforests shelter more than half of the world's 1,000 mountain gorillas. Gorillas share 98 percent of their DNA with humans, and they can catch the same respiratory viruses that humans do.

   With the world on pause, park rangers venture out to care for the gorillas, using face masks and hand sanitizer to avoid infecting these creatures with the virus that keeps the people inside.

8.

Sounders of wild boars haunt the abandoned streets of Haifa, Israel, and other cosmopolitan centers that border the shrinking forests where boars make their grassy nests. They do this from time to time, usually at night.

But with people inside, boars roam during the daytime, too. They snuffle as they overturn garbage cans and root through gardens. Sometimes they block roads, casting huge shadows. The boars don't mean to be destructive. They're just hungry and smell an opportunity to eat without people telling them to shoo.

9.

From the sky, the canaled city of Venice looks like a fish, floating in a lagoon. Most of the time, you can't see what lives in its brackish waters, as noisy boats speed through, churning up mud. But with its gondolas and motorboat taxis moored, Venice's waters turn nearly translucent.

A raft of ducks paddle across the Grand Canal. The sun glints off the silvery backs of a school of tiny fish—anchovies, perhaps? An octopus spreads its tentacles like a hand, feeling its way along the canal floor. A lone jellyfish glides serenely beneath the looking-glass waters.

10.

A colony of sea lions emerge from coastal waters in Mar del Plata, Argentina, and flop on the sand of a seaside resort. They do this day after day—resting on quays, snoring, enjoying a respite from fishing trawlers.

    With so few people out, the sea lions push further into town. They saunter about, eyeing shuttered souvenir stores. The shelter from the wind comforts these nearly 800-pound water mammals, who sunbathe in parking lots like rocks in a sea.

11.

Spring peepers look like tree bark and sing like sleigh bells. Every spring in Maine and east of the Mississippi River, these small frogs slip out from their frozen winter sleep, an army of amphibians trilling songs for mates as they make ready for their seasonal migration. They journey over logs, leaves, and roads to ponds where females lay their eggs.

With so few cars, more of these paperclip-sized frogs than usual cross the road without mishap.

12.

Urban coyotes live along the edges of American cities in forests or woody patches of land. Unlike their prairie and desert kin, they like to hunt at night, when there are fewer humans out and about than in the daytime.

Because the people are inside, day is as serene as night, and packs of coyotes can stroll along avenues in broad daylight. In San Francisco, a coyote trots along the beach with a view of the Golden Gate Bridge. In New York City, coyote pups born in a Bronx graveyard peek out from a ditch beneath a mausoleum—a welcome sign of life.

EPILOGUE

The pause undertaken to slow the spread of COVID-19 began in Wuhan, China, in early 2020. Soon after, the people of northern Italy stayed inside, followed by other regions and countries around the world. Some paused more fully than others. Scientists named this period the "anthropause," because we live in an epoch called the Anthropocene. Our time is the first in which humans' effects on the planet are as strong as natural ones.

The anthropause taught people something exciting about the connections between humans and animals. It has shown us that ecosystems and wildlife can rebound if the right environmental conditions are achieved—look how quickly the wild world responded when humans took a step back and lived more modestly. Without global cooperation, however, in all likelihood, the human factors that create stress for wildlife will return.

Some wildlife didn't fare so well during the pause, especially those animals that have become dependent on humans for food. In Lopburi, Thailand, dozens of macaque monkeys, accustomed to handouts from pilgrims, brawled in the street over what was believed to be a yogurt container. Not all went well for the mountain gorillas in Uganda. With fewer tourists on safari, the gorillas were more vulnerable to poachers because there was no one to witness the crime of killing them. Then there were the sea turtles, who generally thrived on uncrowded beaches, but without enough wildlife biologists available to monitor them in places like Costa Rica and the Dominican Republic, poachers could make off with turtle eggs.

It's fun to think that the creatures in this book were out having adventures while people were inside. Maybe they were. But when possible they naturally expand their habitats in search of food, or more space. And this time, there was more space available. And safer roads for crossing.

So what's next?

It will take international cooperation to make big changes, but each of us individually can slow down, make more room for one another, and create safe spaces for wildlife to thrive in our neighborhoods, and for us to flourish alongside them.

Scientists and volunteers are building wildlife bridges over roads to allow creatures safe passage. Perhaps "critter crossings" can go underground. Some countries are already creating these structures: tunnels for turtles or toads, a crab bridge, rope bridges for squirrels, an elephant underpass, a land bridge for mountain lions.

Many other cohabitation efforts are also under way, and we can help. We can rope off parts of recreational areas during animals' short breeding periods. If we turn down city lights at night, migrating birds won't become disoriented and crash into windows. By opening up wildlife corridors between countries, we can enable animals to follow their ancient migration paths. We can establish more marine protected areas to keep ocean life safe.

We can all help combat climate change. But we need big companies (and small ones) to do their part as well: stop cutting down forests, which causes habitat loss. Support sustainable fishing. Support the preservation of wetlands. Minimize the use of fossil fuels and plastic materials that end up in the bellies of wildlife. Remember that when wildlife is healthy, humans are healthy.

What can you do right, right now? Be a citizen scientist. Volunteer locally to help wildlife in your hometown.

And please, never feed wild animals.

NOTES ON HABITATS, BIOMES, AND WILDLIFE BEHAVIOR

You may have noticed the variety of **habitats** where creatures in this book live. A habitat is the home where a particular organism lives and where it can find the things it needs to survive, like food, water, shelter, and space.

A **biome** refers to the organisms that live in a particular region of the world, and the characteristics of the area, for example the type of soil, or amount of available sunlight in a mountain range or a city. The inter-action of organisms living together under particular environmental elements is called an ecosystem. The numbers and types of biomes differ depending upon the source. The American Museum of Natural History highlights nine in their Hall of Biodiversity: tundra; desert; temperate boreal forest; tropical forest; grassland and savanna; coral reef and coastal wetlands; freshwater wetlands, rivers, and lakes; oceans; and islands.

What is your habitat and biome? What wildlife live near you? How do you interact with your ecosystem?

Here are the ones that appear in this book:

2. Sika deer are native to East Asia (although they are found elsewhere, too.). The deer in this book live in a 1,500-plus-acre public park in Nara, Japan, that has **grassland** and trees like pine trees, cherry trees, and maple.

3. Wild giant pandas' natural habitat is **temperate forests** in the mountains of China.

Flamingos like to roost and nest in wetlands. **Wetlands** are formed by both land and water and can be made up of saltwater or freshwater and a variety of vegetation. The flamingos in this book stop to rest in Navi Mumbai, India but you can find them in the wild in other **tropical** environments.

1. Different types of kangaroos live in varied environments in Australia. The one in this book in all likelihood lived in the Adelaide Hills in southern Australia, where there is **bushland** and **woodlands**.

5. The sea turtles in this book—olive ridley and hawksbill— nest on coastline beaches and spend most of their lives in **tropical** or **subtropical ocean waters**.

6. The lions in this book live in the dry **savanna** in Kruger National Park in South Africa. Their habitat is a mix of grasses and trees.

7. The mountain gorillas in the Bwindi Impenetrable National Park in Uganda, and those in the Virunga Mountains, which connect Uganda, the Democratic Republic of Congo, and Rwanda, live in **high altitude forests**, anywhere from 8,000 to 13,000 feet above sea level.

8. Wild boars range around the edges of many cities. They adapt to a variety of habitats, from **deciduous forests** to **grasslands** and more. The boars in Haifa, Israel have become such regular visitors that some say they are no longer wild. But they are.

9. The city of Venice, Italy sits in a **lagoon**, which is a shallow body of water. The Venetian lagoon is considered the largest **wetland** in the Mediterranean. Salt marshes, grassy sandbanks, mudflats, rivers and sea, fresh-water and saltwater mingle, creating an environment for a variety of wildlife and birds. The appearance of the octopus was very unusual.

10. Sea lions are found along many coastlines, but the ones in this book are called South American sea lions. They live in the **ocean** along the South American coastline, and some nearby islands. The ones reported to have wandered further than usual into town were seen in the port of Mar del Plata, Argentina.

11. The spring peepers in this story live in Maine, but they are commonly found in the eastern parts of Canada and east of the Mississippi in the United States. They live in moist, **wooded areas** or **grassy lowlands** near **ponds** and **swamps**.

12. Highly adaptable coyotes are found throughout North and Central America in **prairies**, **deserts**, **forests**, **mountains**, and, like the ones in this book, on the outskirts of large **cities**, and sometimes even in city centers.

Note: Scientists often update their statistics and studies, so it is important to look up the most recent information about animals' numbers, habitats, and behaviors.

SOME FURTHER RESOURCES

World Wildlife Fund:
   https://www.worldwildlife.org/teaching-resources
Wildlife Conservation Society:
   https://www.wcs.org/
The Cornell Lab of Ornithology:
   https://www.birds.cornell.edu/home/
The National Audubon Society:
   https://www.audubon.org/
American Museum of Natural History: Biodiversity resources
   https://www.amnh.org/exhibitions/permanent/biodiversity/educator-resources
National Geographic Kids: Habitats:
   https://kids.nationalgeographic.com/explore/nature/habitats/

ACKNOWLEDGMENTS

The term "**anthropause**" first appeared in this article: Rutz, C., Loretto, M.C., Bates, A.E. et al. "COVID-19 Lockdown Allows Researchers to Quantify the Effects of Human Activity on Wildlife." Nat Ecol Evol 4, 1156–1159 (2020).

Special thanks to Dr. Matthias-Claudio Loretto, who spoke with me about his research on the anthropause; and to Dr. Peter Mahoney, wildlife biologist at NOAA Alaska Fisheries Science Center, Dr. Catherine Czaya, Ms. Sasha Swift, science teacher, and research editor Alexis Sottile for expert fact-checking assistance.